DBT Therapy Workbook for Kids 8-12

Effective Exercises to Manage Emotions, Improve Interpersonal Effectiveness, Distress Tolerance and Mindfulness

By

Anthony N.

Wisdom Publishing

© Copyright 2023 by Wisdom Publishing- All rights reserved.

Without the prior written permission of the Publisher, no part of this publication may be stored in a retrieval system, replicated or transferred in any form or medium, digital, scanning, recording, printing, mechanical or otherwise, except as permitted under 1976 United States Copyright Act, section 107 or 108. Permission concerns should be directed to the publisher's permission department.

Legal Notice

This book is copyright protected. It is only to be used for personal purposes. Without the author's or publisher's permission, you cannot paraphrase, quote, copy, distribute, sell or change any part of the information in this book.

Disclaimer Notice

This book is written and published independently. Please keep in mind that the material in this publication is solely for educational and entertainment purposes. All efforts have been made to provide authentic, up-to-date, trustworthy and comprehensive information. There are no express or implied assurances. The purpose of this book's material is to assist readers in having a better understanding of the subject matter. The activities, information and exercises are provided solely for self-help information. This book is not intended to replace expert psychologists, legal, financial or other guidance. If you require counseling, please get in touch with a qualified professional.

By reading this text, the reader accepts that the author will not be held liable for any damages, indirectly or directly, experienced due to the use of the information included herein, particularly, but not limited to, omissions, errors or inaccuracies. As a reader, you are accountable for your decisions, actions and consequences.

About the Author

Anthony N. is a certified Psychologist with eight years of experience. Throughout his career, he has helped clients with a broad range of issues. He has collaborated in various coaching programs at the executive level.

He is well-equipped in conventional therapy practices as he has studied them in depth and put that knowledge into practice for many years. He treats his patients and clients with compassion, empathy and understanding. He has vast knowledge in handling mental health issues, such as depression, anxiety, mood disorders, stress management, trauma and PTSD.

Contents

Note to Parents 5

Introduction 6

Chapter 1: Have You Met Alicia? 7

Chapter 2: Big Emotions! 15

Chapter 3: A Friendly World! 27

Chapter 4: Be Aware! 39

Chapter 5: Stay Calm! 50

Goodbye Message 62

Note to Parents

Thank you for choosing this excellent book written and designed to let your child learn Dialectical Behavior Therapy (DBT) skills. DBT skills provide practical tools for emotional regulation, cherishing healthy relationships and mindfulness.

DBT Therapy involves Managing Emotions and Improving Interpersonal Effectiveness, Distress Tolerance and Mindfulness to help your kid find calmness and tranquility.

As you read this storybook with your child, you will find some activities that require adult involvement and guidance. I encourage you to participate alongside your kid to create an interactive and meaningful experience.

By reading together, you can help your child understand the DBT skills presented in the book. It would be helpful if you encourage open discussions, share your experiences and guide your child through all activities so that they grasp the concepts.

This book provides a supportive framework for a child's emotional growth. You can provide a supportive and secure atmosphere for your kid to explore emotions, build resilience and develop life skills. This book helps promote emotional intelligence, so I hope you will like it.

Introduction

This book reveals Alicia and Benny follow through an Enchanted Forest on an exciting adventure. A charming young girl named Alicia learns many skills while searching for a missing key to happiness and tranquility. This book inspires bold readers like you to embrace your originality, generosity and self-discovery. See how Alicia uses the DBT techniques she picks up throughout the journey to find her lost key and open up a world of joy, compassion and lifelong learning. Let's begin!

Chapter 1: Have You Met Alicia?

Meet Alicia and Benny!

Alicia was an inquisitive, lively girl with curling red hair and glowing attitude. She loved having travels to learn and make friends. Alicia's closest companion was a mischievous bunny. He was Benny. His disposition was cheerful and pleasant.

Alicia and Benny were playing outdoors one winter morning when they heard other youngsters talking about a missing key in an Enchanted Forest. The key was unusual. This was intended to open a portal to happiness and peace. They were interested in locating it. The Enchanted Forest included tall trees, beautiful streams and talking creatures.

They encountered several problems on their way to the jungle. Alicia sometimes wanted to go home and Benny sometimes became annoyed. But they always supported each other.

Alicia and Benny Want to Meet You Too!

Now that you know, Alicia and Benny, they want to meet you! Everyone has a unique tale to offer. Alicia and Benny want to know your tale.

What are your favorite activities, animals and good memories? Alicia sees you as a fearless child like her. She feels that sharing tales and learning about others may foster a nice and pleasant environment.

Think about what makes you distinctive. Alicia and Benny eagerly await an opportunity to learn about your distinctive qualities.

Who Am I?

Draw your face and fill colors.

A Self-Portrait

Let Alicia see how you look. Draw yourself!

Wonderful Things I Can Do

Tell Alicia about some amazing things you can do.

My Family and Friends

Alicia wants to know the people you love. Write their names.

Name: _____   **Date:** _____

| Grandmother | Grandfather | Mom |

| Dad | Brother | Sister |

| Friends |

Meeting Benny

Meet Benny, color him and tell him if you have a special friend like him.

Let's find out how Alicia and Benny found the key!

Chapter 2: Big Emotions!

As Alicia and Benny ventured deeper into the Enchanted Forest, they stumbled upon a meadow filled with colorful flowers. It was so beautiful that Alicia and Benny couldn't help but feel a rush of joy and excitement.

However, just as quickly, her emotions shifted when she noticed a sign saying, "Lost key seekers must solve the first hurdle named 'Emotion Express Rapids' to move forward."

As Alicia and Benny approached the Emotion Express Rapids, they found themselves overwhelmed by strong emotions like anger, sadness, or fear. They needed to practice emotion regulation and learn how to identify and manage their emotions effectively. By expressing their feelings in healthy ways, they could safely cross the rapids.

Alicia felt a mix of frustration and determination. Being the wise little rabbit, Benny reminded Alicia about the importance of going through the land of emotions.

"Emotions are like waves in the ocean," Benny said.

"Sometimes they're big and strong and other times gentle and calm. Like riding a wave, we can learn to control our emotions without getting overwhelmed."

Alicia took a moment to acknowledge her feelings and reminded herself that she could handle them. She closed her eyes and imagined herself exploring that land, feeling each rise and fall exhilaration. She felt more in control of her emotions and ready to face the hurdles ahead.

We have learned the following:

- Sometimes we feel big emotions, like happiness or sadness.
- Emotions are like colorful flowers that show how we feel inside.
- It's okay to have different feelings and emotions.
- We can learn to control our feelings.
- Taking a moment to calm down can help us feel better.
- It's important to understand and talk about our feelings.
- Trying our best and being brave helps us face challenges.
- The Enchanted Forest has taught us that emotions are special.

Is It a Good Feeling?

Benny helped Alicia identify good feelings. Color the areas that have good feelings. It will help you to identify good feelings. With good feelings, we can face anything in life.

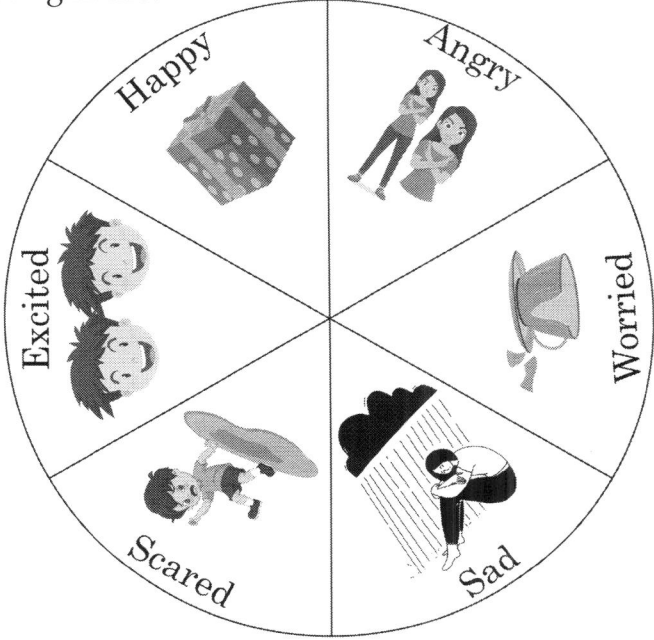

Can You Guess?

Benny made different faces to teach Alicia how to guess the emotions. Can you guess the name of these emotions? Yes, You can! Let's try.

Finding My Emotions

Tell Alicia how wonderful you are at finding emotions.

```
Y X A R C U R I O U S S
F R U S T R A T E D K A
C E S U R P R I S E D D
A E X C I T E D D D V S
L I P A L C A N G R Y Q
M H A P P Y P R O U D U
J P T Q S C A R E D W E
W C C N E R V O U S F X
```

HAPPY	**SURPRISED**
SAD	**PROUD**
EXCITED	**FRUSTRATED**
ANGRY	**NERVOUS**
SCARED	**CURIOUS**
CALM	

How am I Feeling?

What does your frustration look like? Can you draw it?

I am a Turtle!

Whenever you feel overwhelmed like Alicia, become a turtle:

1. Understand your emotions.
2. Pause and reflect.
3. Go inside.
4. Reemerge when you feel calm.
5. Consider possible solutions.

How am I Feeling Today?

So, how was your day today? How are you feeling?

It Makes Me Feel

We want to be more sure of our feelings. So, be honest and name a person, thing, or place related to the following emotions.

5		It makes me feel upset.
4		It makes me feel happy.
3		It makes me feel nervous.
2		It makes me feel excited.
1		It bothers me.

Let's Do Some Exercise

When you feel overwhelming emotions, try these fun exercises. Benny taught these to Alicia.

3 Pushups

5 Jumping Jacks

5 Lunges

10 Times Raise Your Arms

10 Marches

10 Frog Jumps

Positive Talk

Do you know how we do positive talk? Let Benny teach you.

- If you lose a game, say," I had a lot of fun."

- I am a positive thinker.

- If you are confused, just talk to someone.

- My family is happy that I am a positive thinker and solve my problems with positive talk.

- Positive thinkers focus on the good things.

- If you are disappointed, say," It is fine."

What Should I Do?

If you are feeling frustrated, follow the steps.

I should

| Sit | Fold hands | Breathe |
| Drink water | Do some counting | Talk to someone |

Here we go!

You have learned about your big emotions. Alicia would be happy that you have learned to control your emotions like her.

Let's explore the Forest and go with Alicia one step ahead.

Chapter 3: A Friendly World!

Alicia and Benny arrived at the Friendship Forest Fiesta, a joyful celebration of friendship. But they didn't know anyone there.

In Friendship Forest Fiesta, Alicia and Benny faced the second hurdle: Relationship Riddle. Alicia and Benny met some talking animals who were having conflicts with one another. They needed something useful such as 'interpersonal effectiveness' to learn how to communicate their needs, listen empathetically and solve problems together. By using effective communication, they could help the animals resolve their conflicts and move forward.

Alicia did not know what to do. Then they met Oliver, a wise owl. Oliver shared the secret to cross this hurdle.

The secret was:

- Being kind, listening and showing interest in others.
- To treat others with respect and listen when they talk.
- To express your thoughts and feelings honestly without hurting them.

Alicia and Benny solved the hurdle. They used their new skills, introducing themselves, asking questions and listening attentively. They made everyone friends.

Alicia, Benny and their new friends created beautiful connections. As their adventure continued, they knew they could overcome any challenge and make the world happier.

Let's use the secret of Oliver and become a social bee!

My Friends

Alicia and Benny taught all the animals that friendship is a special bond that brings hearts together. True friendship is a treasure that lasts forever. True friends feel like the sunshine on a cloudy day, bringing warmth and brightness. A good friend is like a mirror, reflecting our best qualities and cheering us on. What does friendship mean to you?

The meaning of friendship for me is...

Say Nice Things!

It's important to say nice things to each other because:

- ✓ Kind words make people happy.
- ✓ Saying nice things strengthens friendships.
- ✓ Nice words spread happiness.
- ✓ We can inspire and encourage others with our kind words.
- ✓ Saying nice things creates a positive and kind world.

So, let's use our words to be kind and make each other happy!

Instructions:

1. Gather all your friends in the circle.
2. One friend will say something to the friend next to them.
3. That friend will then say something nice to the person next to them.
4. Keep doing this until you reach the friend from where it all started.

My Friendship Toolbox

In the forest, all animals were having conflict with one another. Conflict is when people have different ideas or feelings and it causes problems. It's like a disagreement or argument. When conflicts happen, we need to find a way to solve them and understand each other's feelings. It's important to be kind and respectful when trying to fix conflicts.

Choose something from the following toolbox whenever you have a conflict with your friend.

- ✓ Keep yourself calm
- ✓ Apologize
- ✓ Take turns
- ✓ Be kind and empathetic

What would you choose from the above toolbox?

_____

What should I do?

When resolving a conflict with someone, what should we do?

- ✓ Put a star sticker in front of positive behavior for conflict resolution.
- ✓ Cross the negative behavior for conflict resolution.

Stay Calm	Find Solutions Together:
Use Kind Words	Apologize and Forgive
Listen Carefully	Use Active Listening
Blaming and Accusing	Take Turns
Interrupting	Seek Help from Adults
Using Mean Words	Show Empathy
Holding Grudges	Hitting or Hurting Others
Being Rude	Yelling or Shouting
Gossiping	Running Away
Express your feelings and needs	Ignoring Others

Be Assertive!

Alicia taught animals to be assertive. Being assertive means expressing yourself confidently and respectfully. It's about speaking up for yourself and sharing your thoughts, feelings and needs without being mean or bossy. When you're assertive, you stand up for yourself and communicate clearly. It's important to be assertive and not let others take advantage of you while also considering the feelings of others.

Read the following situations and help them how they can be assertive in handling situations.

Two friends want to use the same art supplies. 	A child disagrees with their parent about bedtime rules. 
Two siblings argue about who gets to choose the TV show. 	A stranger approaches a child at the park and asks personal questions. 
Two friends have different ideas for a game. 	In a group project, a child feels their ideas are not being heard. 

Saying 'No'

Benny took the front seat to teach animals that in friendship, sometimes we must decide when to say "no" or "yes." Here's a simple way to understand it:

Saying "No":

- ✓ Saying " no " is okay when something feels wrong or unsafe.
- ✓ Say "no" if someone wants you to break a rule or do something you don't want.
- ✓ Trust yourself and say "no" when taking care of yourself is important.

Saying "Yes":

- ✓ Say "yes" when a friend asks you to play or do something fun together.
- ✓ If someone needs your help or kindness, saying "yes" can make them happy.
- ✓ Saying "yes" when it feels right can make your friendship stronger.

In this activity:

- ✓ The red sign indicates the time to say no.
- ✓ The yellow sign indicates a warning.
- ✓ The green sign indicates saying yes to friendship.

Read the situation and add color to see whether it's time to say no, a warning, or yes to friendship.

Two friends want to use the same art supplies.	
A child disagrees with their parent about bedtime rules.	
Two siblings argue about who gets to choose the TV show.	
A stranger approaches a child at the park and asks personal questions.	
Two friends have different ideas for a game.	
In a group project, a child feels their ideas are not being heard.	

Healthy or Unhealthy Relationship

A healthy relationship is when people treat each other with kindness, respect and fairness. It's like a friendship where both people feel safe, happy and supported in a healthy relationship.

On the other hand, an unhealthy relationship doesn't feel good. It's when someone is mean, hurts your feelings, or makes you scared in an unhealthy relationship.

Do you want to know how Alicia taught animals the difference between healthy and unhealthy relationship? Do this activity and tell whether it is a healthy or unhealthy relationship.

True/false

	T	F
• In a healthy relationship, we treat each other with kindness and respect.	☐	☐
• Healthy friendships make us feel happy, safe and supported.	☐	☐
• Good friends do not listen to us or care about our feelings.	☐	☐
• Healthy relationships involve sharing, compromising and taking turns.	☐	☐
• Good friends do not encourage us to be ourselves and celebrate our uniqueness.	☐	☐
• In healthy relationships, we solve problems by talking and understanding each other.	☐	☐
• Healthy relationships allow us to respect each other's boundaries.	☐	☐
• Good friends apologize when they make mistakes and try to make things right.	☐	☐
• Healthy relationships are built on loyalty.	☐	☐
• Healthy relationships make us feel sad, scared, or uncomfortable.	☐	☐
• Healthy relationships involve bullying, name-calling, or teasing.	☐	☐
• Healthy relationships make us feel ignored or left out.	☐	☐
• Healthy relationships involve fighting, yelling, or physical harm.	☐	☐
• Unhealthy relationships involve lying, cheating, or being dishonest.	☐	☐

From Oliver's (the wise owl) secret, we have learned to:

- ✓ Be kind, listen and help each other.
- ✓ Share and take turns.
- ✓ Respect feelings, thoughts and personal space.
- ✓ Communicate openly and honestly.
- ✓ Solve problems together calmly.
- ✓ Support and celebrate each other.
- ✓ Show empathy and understanding.
- ✓ Be trustworthy and keep promises.
- ✓ Resolve conflicts peacefully.

Oliver gave wonderful advice to Alicia and us too. Now it's time to see what comes next.

Chapter 4: Be Aware!

Alicia and Benny came across a small clearing where they noticed a family of squirrels busily collecting acorns. Alicia watched in awe as the squirrels moved with such focus and attention. She asked Benny how they were so good at what they were doing.

Benny smiled and explained, *"They're practicing something called mindfulness."*

Mindfulness means paying attention to the present moment without judgment. When we're mindful, we can focus on what we're doing and enjoy it fully.

Here comes the third hurdle, Mindfulness Maze. Alicia and Benny encountered a maze filled with distractions and overwhelming thoughts.

They needed to practice mindfulness, focusing on the present moment and observing their surroundings without judgment. By staying mindful, they could move closer to find the lost key.

We should also learn this wonderful trick. Let's do it!

Mindful Breathing

Mindful breathing helped Alicia and Benny calm down and feel peaceful. It's a great way to be aware and feel better when stressed or worried.

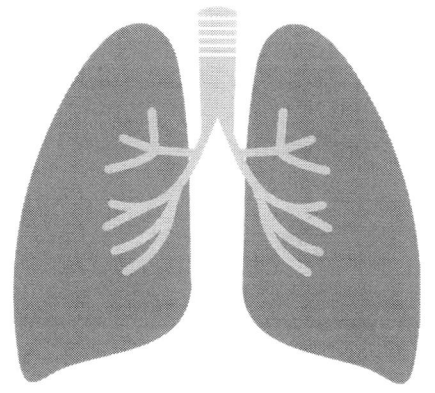

1. Breathing Power

First, get yourself ready to breathe deeply. Write '8' on paper. Trace the number by breathing deeply while drawing the first half and gently exhaling while drawing the second half.

2. Deep Breaths

Feel the warmth of your hands on the belly and breathe deeply. Inhale and expand your belly. Exhale twice to lower your belly. Do it ten times. Try this when you're upset.

3. Use Timer

Set a one-minute timer. Breathe in and out until the timer rings. Listen and feel everything. Take note of your thoughts.

Sun Breathing

Trace the sunbeams with your fingertips as you breathe!

Mindful Living

Mindful living means being aware of what is happening in the present moment just like Alicia noticed about squirrels. It's about paying attention to our thoughts, feelings and actions. Practicing mindfulness allows us to enjoy each moment and make the most of our experiences.

1. One moment

Set a one-minute timer. Focus on what you hear, smell and touch and focus on the now.

2. Spider Senses

For two minutes, become a "spider" and examine your room with superpowers. In this state, you'll be able to notice everything. What are the things you notice?

3. Focus Tree

Spend two minutes studying a tree outside. See all of its details. Examine its leaves, trunk, lines and hues. Smell it and tell me what you feel.

Follow the Steps!

Here is another wonderful way of breathing.

Take three deep breaths and look up at the sky.

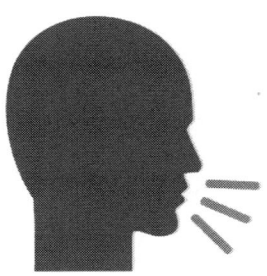

Breathe down to your shoes.

Exhale up to the top of your head.

Be Aware!

Being aware means paying attention to what is happening around and inside us. It's like using our senses to notice the world and how we feel. By being aware, we can fully enjoy and understand the things happening in our lives.

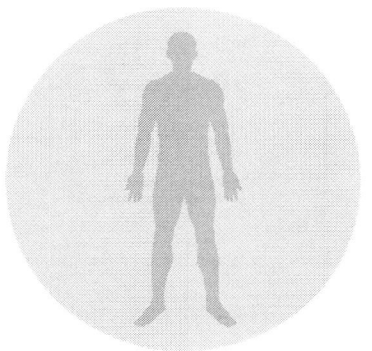

1. Scan Your Body

Relax your shoulders for 10 seconds. Ten seconds later, squeeze your stomach and Relax. Then, tense and relax your entire body.

2. Trace Your Fingers

Open your hand and look at your starfish fingers. Trace all of your fingers. Do the same with your other hand. This is a great nighttime exercise. It's rhythmic.

3. Blindfolded Time Begins

Choose the five fruits that fit in your palm. Taste them one by one while being blindfolded. This is a tasting game. Tell me how does it feel in your mouth.

Colorful Breathing

Imagine your worries as a hue. Breathe deeply and release your anxieties. For example, imagine exhaling red for three counts. To get yourself relaxed, inhale a soothing and joyful color like blue. To make yourself happy, inhale green. Does it make you smile? Inhale for three counts. Repeat until your troubles are gone and you're filled with a beautiful, peaceful light.

Alicia and Benny followed this trick. Are you ready to calm down, focus and relax?

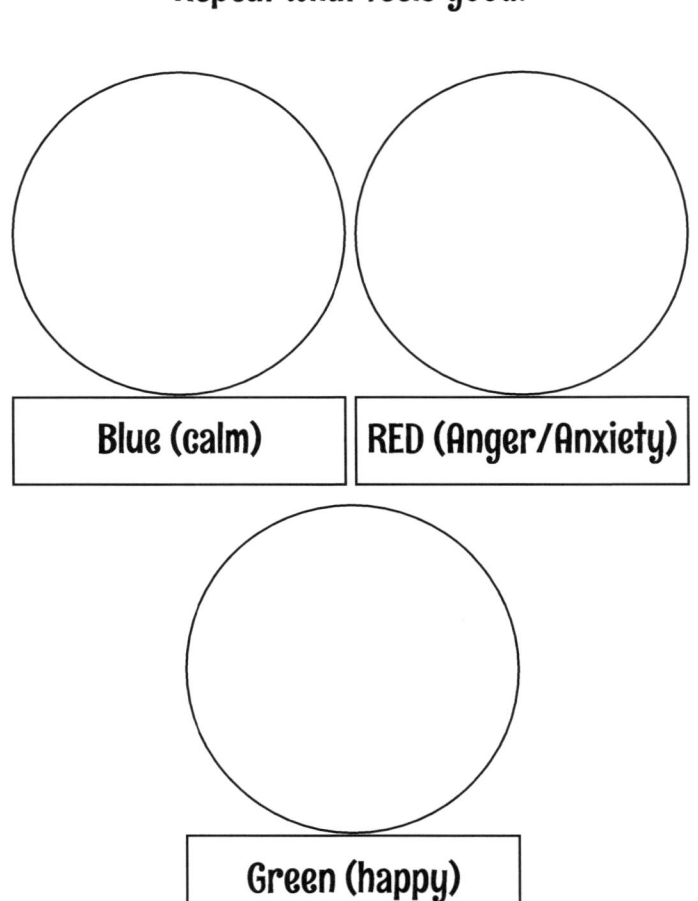

Distract Yourself

Stress is a feeling of being overwhelmed or worried. It can happen when we have too much to do, or something bothers us. It is important to distract ourselves. So, which activities would you like to do to distract yourself from stress?

- ☐ Pay attention to something you need to do or eat something you like.
- ☐ Engage in sports.
- ☐ Watch TV.
- ☐ Find something to do.
- ☐ Create or draw something.
- ☐ Spend time with family.
- ☐ Play with cards.
- ☐ Read magazine.
- ☐ Do crossword problems or Sudoku.
- ☐ Exercise.
- ☐ Count to 10; count out the situation by letting it alone for a while: Yell "No!"
- ☐ Count anything you see in a picture, poster, or out of the window.
- ☐ Sing a song.
- ☐ Keep the ice in your hand or your mouth.

Are Your Senses Aware?

We can use our eyes, ears, nose, tongue and skin. We can discover new things and enjoy the world's wonders like Alicia and Benny by paying attention to our senses.

Using your senses to become aware of the world around you can be a fun and exciting experience!

1. Can you feel the warmth of the sun on your skin?

2. Can you taste the sweetness of a juicy apple?

3. Can you smell the delicious scent of freshly baked cookies?

4. Can you feel the softness of a kitten's fur when you pet it?

5. Can you notice the ticklish sensation of grass beneath your bare feet?

6. Can you hear the gentle sound of waves crashing at the beach?

7. Can you feel the cool breeze on your face on a windy day?

8. Can you taste the refreshing coldness of an ice cream cone?

9. Can you smell the fragrant flowers in a garden?

10. Can you notice the texture of the sand between your toes?

11. Can you hear leaves rustling as the wind blows through the trees?

12. Can you feel the weight of a smooth pebble in your hand?

13. Can you taste the tanginess of a freshly squeezed lemon?

14. When you tap a drum with your fingers, can you notice the vibration and sound?

So like Alicia, we learned from the squirrels:

Mindfulness is about:

- ✓ Using our senses to notice the world around us.
- ✓ We can be mindful by focusing on breathing or what we see, hear, smell, taste and touch.
- ✓ It helps us stay calm, be present and enjoy the moment.
- ✓ Mindfulness is like being a curious explorer of our own lives.

Remember, practicing mindfulness can make us happy and help us appreciate the little things in life!

Chapter 5: Stay Calm!

Alicia and Benny reached a point in the forest where they needed to cross a deep and wide river. Alicia was a little nervous because she didn't know how to swim and the water looked cold and fast. Benny noticed her worry and reminded her of a special technique called "calm breathing."

"Calm breathing is like blowing colorful bubbles," Benny explained to Alicia, "Take a deep breath and fill your tummy like a balloon. Then, slowly breathe out through your mouth, just like we do to blow bubbles. This helps us feel focused and calm."

Alicia followed Benny just like a good girl and took a deep breath. She felt a sense of calm wash over her and her worries about crossing the river started to fade away.

With renewed confidence, Alicia and Benny built a sturdy raft out of fallen tree branches and safely crossed the river together.

As Alicia and Benny ventured through the Enchanted Forest, they encountered a pile of leaves. Alicia noticed a sparkle of light peeking through the leaves. Curiosity sparked in her eyes as she carefully brushed away the leaves, revealing a magnificent key hidden beneath. It was the key they had been searching for, waiting to unlock exciting happiness.

We should also learn and practice what Benny told Alicia. Let's do it!

Become A Turtle

Behaving like a turtle means finding a quiet place, taking slow breaths and moving calmly. It helped Alicia and Benny stay calm and patient and tolerate the distress, just like a turtle in its shell.

Triangle Breathing

You can keep yourself calm in tense situations with triangle breathing.

Instruction:

1. Breathe in through your nose, counting to three.
2. Hold your breath for three counts.
3. Breathe out through your mouth, counting to three.
4. Pause without breathing for three counts.
5. Repeat these steps a few times.
6. Sit quietly, breathe in (3), hold (3), breathe out (3), pause (3). Repeat.

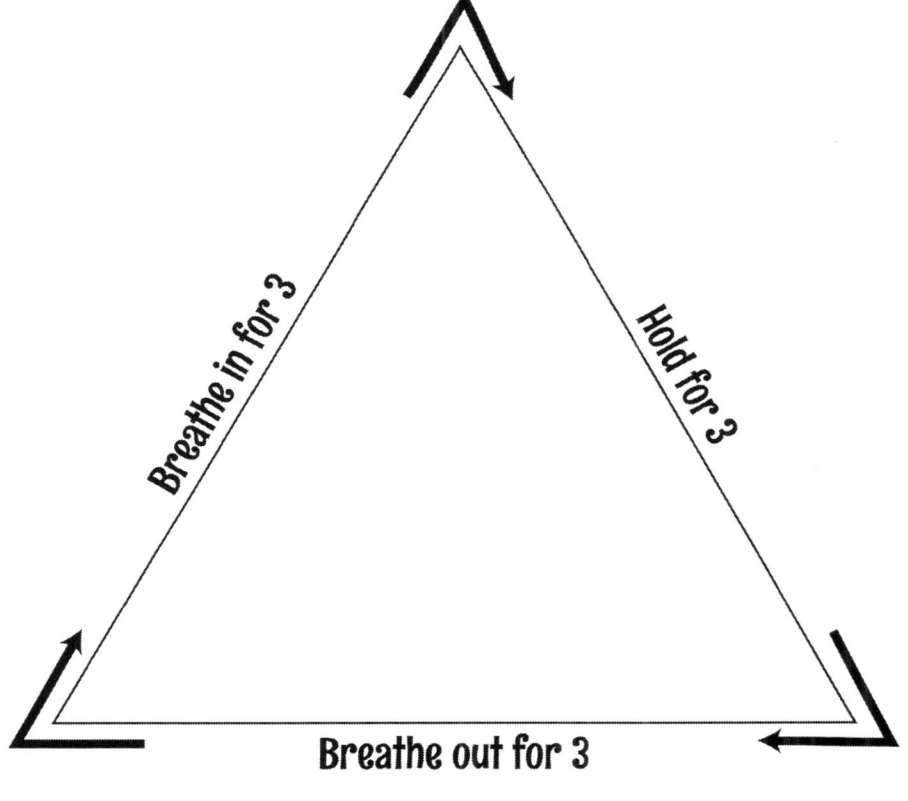

Do Some Stretching

The child's pose is a relaxing stretch that can help your body feel calm and peaceful. Enjoy the gentle stretch with Alicia and Benny and take deep breaths while in the pose.

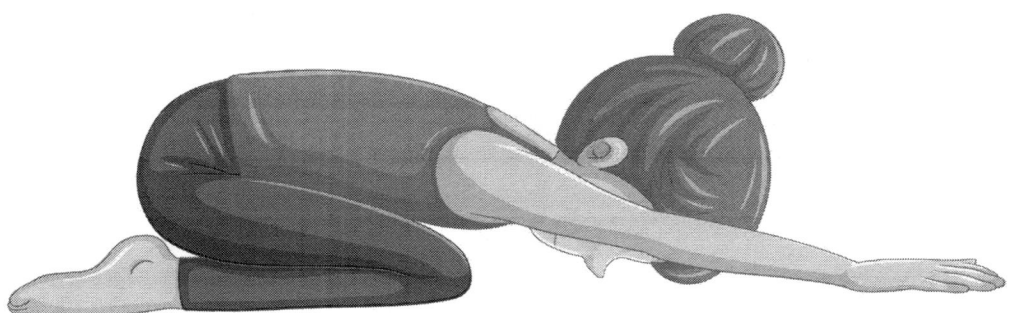

Instructions:

1. Find a comfortable spot on the floor where you can kneel.
2. Sit back gently onto your heels. Imagine your forehead gradually approaching the ground.
3. Extend your arms straight ahead, like you're trying to reach for something in the distance.
4. Take a deep breath, then exhale slowly, releasing any tension.
5. Stay in this peaceful position for a little while. Feel the gentle stretch in your back, shoulders and arms.
6. Get back to the original position and feel calm.

5-Seconds Breathing

Breathing should feel calm and natural. Take your time and try to make each breath last for four counts. This 5-second breathing exercise will help you remain calm and focused whenever you feel stressed.

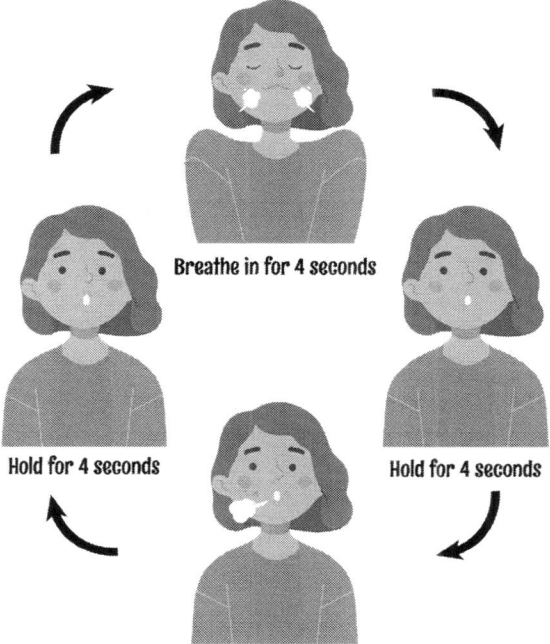

Instructions:

1. Find a comfortable place to do this exercise.
2. Take a deep breath.
3. Hold your breath for a moment, counting to five.
4. Slowly exhale, counting to five.
5. Pause without breathing for a moment.
6. Repeat these steps, counting to five for each breath.

Time to Relax Your Muscles

Muscle relaxation is when we make our bodies feel loose and calm. We can do it by taking deep breaths and imagining our muscles getting soft and relaxed. It helped Alicia and Benny feel more peaceful and relaxed, like a sleepy cat.

Word Search

O	V	E	R	W	H	E	L	M	E	D	A
I	M	P	A	T	I	E	N	C	E	D	N
N	E	R	V	O	U	S	N	E	S	S	G
I	R	R	I	T	A	T	I	O	N	X	E
L	W	Y	A	N	X	I	E	T	Y	B	R
R	E	S	T	L	E	S	S	N	E	S	S
F	R	U	S	T	R	A	T	I	O	N	N
W	O	R	R	I	E	D	B	S	Y	N	U

Find these words.

ANXIETY

NERVOUSNESS

WORRIED

OVERWHELMED

FRUSTRATION

IRRITATION

ANGER

IMPATIENCE

RESTLESSNESS

UNEASINESS

Cultivate Optimism

Alicia and Benny were optimistic about finding the lost key. An optimistic mindset involves looking at the brighter side of things, expecting positive outcomes, maintaining a hopeful attitude, cultivating optimism in your life and adding vibrant colors to this image.

Move Your Body!

Staying active and moving your body to stay healthy and strong is important. For now, add vibrant colors to this image and promise yourself that you will move your body whenever you get anxious.

Write a Gratitude Journal

A gratitude journal is a special activity where we write down things we are thankful for daily. It helps us remember the good things in our lives and makes us feel happy. Writing in a gratitude journal is like collecting treasures of joy and appreciation.

What are you grateful for?

You have learned that to remain calm like Alicia and Benny, you should:

- ✓ Take slow, deep breaths when feeling upset or overwhelmed.
- ✓ Close your eyes and imagine a peaceful place or count to ten to help calm down.
- ✓ Remind yourself that things will be okay.
- ✓ Take breaks and do activities you enjoy.
- ✓ Practice mindfulness by focusing on the present moment.
- ✓ Use calming techniques like stretching and exercise.
- ✓ Remember that it's okay to ask for help when you need it.
- ✓ Practice being patient and understanding with yourself and others.

Alicia and Benny have found the lost key of calmness and happiness by adopting the skills we learned in this book. I hope you have also found your key to happiness and success.

Goodbye Message

As we reach the end of this book, I want to remind you of some incredible skills you have learned. These skills will help you live through life with confidence and happiness. Remember to express your feelings using your words, just like magic spells that help others understand you better. Then, please take a deep breath when things feel overwhelming and let it fill you with calm and strength. Being a true friend means listening with your heart and making others feel heard and loved. Finally, keep your mind filled with happy thoughts, like a sky full of colorful balloons and watch as positivity fills your days. As we say goodbye for now, always remember that you are capable of doing incredible things. Keep shining bright and spreading your magic wherever you go!

Made in the USA
Coppell, TX
23 July 2024

35089323R10035